Court of Common Pleas

Court of Common Pleas

Alice Glarden Brand

Mellen Poetry Press
Lewiston/Queenston/Lampeter

Acknowledgments ———————————————

Grateful acknowledgment is extended to Yaddo where many of these
poems were written, and to Laura Schneck for her editing and design.

Poems from this collection have been published in *americas review;
Circles, The Buffalo Women's Journal of Law and Social Policy; Coal
City Review; College Composition and Communication; Confrontation;
Footwork: The Paterson Literary Review; George Washington Review;* ·
*Kalliope; Midwest Quarterly; New Letters; Nimrod; Phoebe; Pleiades;
The Prose Poem; San Fernando Poetry Journal; Slipstream; Teaching
English in the Two-Year College; Texas Journal of Women and the Law;
Wascana; Wordsmith*

Library of Congress Cataloging-in-Publication Data

Brand, Alice Glarden.
   Court of common pleas / Alice G. Brand.
    p. cm.
   ISBN 0-7734-2687-6 (paper)
   I. Title.
   PS3552.R2916C68 1996
   811'.54--dc   96-42393
                                              CIP

Printed in the United States of America

To my grandchildren
Robert Alexander, Madeleine Claire, Errol Brand,
and those yet to be

Contents

Things Women ————————————————

Amusements ————————————————

Court of Common Pleas ——————————————————

Writers in Winter

Do not make fun of me
if I read at breakfast.
no one is here
and I do not want to think of this
my opportunity lost.
it is mine to enter into,
without cutting the forest down,
to trim just what I need until the snow words into spring.
someone is emptying a pail of ice rather mindlessly
and has forgotten that we live below and happen to be
hanging out our sheets and cotton rug.
by afternoon the weather lingers
in a gold swag I cannot touch.

Do not make fun of me if I go to bed early
and do not play music or tell a story
about halvah in Istanbul or aubergine.
I do not mean to lose my appetite
for long evenings of stories.
the images dissolve before they are wrung out.

Do not laugh if I just nod to your holiday
which will be sisterful from the Midwest
and children. a niece and nephews exchange gifts.
imagine what would happen if I really listened.
I would never go anywhere again
but become coiled in this life and
ask your sister's name,
how old she is,
which city in the Midwest, what this holiday is,
and can I come for dinner.

Do not mind if I sleep in the attic,
if I empty my waste basket of old tea bags
and crusts, wipe the base of the
lamp of its routine, the cup I have drained
of its camomile, left there
for finding calm the words I came for.

about my son

at 1 in the afternoon there is still a vast lake
to swim across.
I have not had the kind of training needed.
the water is murky
but no one has lost her life in it.
it is cold and warm.
I cannot wade too far without
pushing my legs up and trying to float.
do I eat the water weeds, take them for hair that
I spread out and shape into an island on which I rest
beneath a pebble sky that so threatens to hurt
I must avoid it even if it means lying to myself and to you.

between us death will starve.
we will not be righteous or arrogant,
but we will not serve him well.
we will provide no occasion for him to come
around the back and feed on our porch,
even scraps in a bowl,
dried and rancid.
we will keep the light on,
the strange steady drip of life.
he will come by in a torn lumber jacket
and look idly around. we will be there
but he will not find us.

slow shoes

whose shadow do I replace in this room?
who was I before me who leaves it just the way I do,
a crumpled tissue, an empty soda can and straw?
she left the restaurant in a rush,
not paying or waving good-bye.

what splendid chaos goes on here that
my desk rubs up against the wall so
ardently I cannot pass? chairs continually part
to the sides as for a dance, carpet
rolled out between songs.
there are papers and a lectern, no books,
no blotter, nothing in the trash
until I throw it there.
I do not erase the coaxings of a literary experience,
its design and numbers, where I meet her belongings
but never her.

who is this person who writes on the board
but leaves no chalk, the unglamorous
waking up from bed, mistakes shaken from the sheets,
a splash of ideas bank along the shore,
foam and seaweed. she left without a turn,
her high heels chipped and scuffed,
a brusque mistress whose swift smell flies
like the curtain I pull across to cover her jottings.

what can I make of her, living scattered in my walls
like disheveled hair? her guests are somewhere,
refusing the missionary position, reveling in hers.
the lawful secrets of fancy, flattery, foreplay,
foreknowledge, foreshadowing, fortune.

who would know that what I have to say
she has had to say, and that all I ever wanted
was to be in this room and listen to her,
to be her needle, her thread and cloth,
to be in the turning and unturning of pages,

the magic arrival of meaning that I can read
and know my destiny from a distance,
from the way she moves her hand along the desk,
her caress on my shoulder, even though I have come in,
even though she is always gone.

the slow run backward

Disease kept me up last night. When I turned
to him and put my face to his mouth,
he thought I wanted to make love.

I wanted instead to suck out his juice and
leave him squirming where he could not
fit easily between life and death.
His legs bridge a cold and flu,
a virus, mono. To test positive
is to develop fever, find purple stains
on my son's thigh
like the autumn within a pine.
I will not let this flash take me
to its logical end which it would do
because my son would not go alone.

It is true that his words never stayed
obediently on the page.
They laughed in your face when
you tried to tame them.
They rose like they were
leaving the country illegally.

The clot that lodged in his spine
no one could avert. If only he is
healthy now, I will stretch
myself across the unrepented.
From this moment on
the sky is in his fingers
the way it used to be.

Taffeta

You have always given me gifts.
On your birthday you have given me gifts,
at my porch lodged between the screen and door,
sometimes over the phone.

How did they arrive?
Did you break in? Tap my wires?
Did the super let you in?
We entered into no special pact.
You did not arrive by default or design.
You pull down the shade
at the swelter of my life.
You flow like cream. You don't count your change
while I shuffle for my wallet.
Tomorrow I will find you in the
smile of a branch and wonder
what is meant by invitations
the origins of which are now obscure

the dried peonies, a lily or
song, things trivial and elusive
that I tell no one about.
Your scent slips under my door like light
and undoes the sadness I accept as home.

I look at the smallest foot soldier
among the army of strangers who
stumble along the road, not knowing why
we are the beneficiary, the beloved.
Everything about us is inauspicious.
We have done little to deserve you.

Soap washes cleaner than us and is more useful,
even at its poorest,
this twig in the forgotten of forests.
We rarely receive something that in some way
we don't have to give back. Especially when
it has been so long and you call,
and your letters ride high
along the Continential Divide.

We are all lost or stolen.
If time were left to its own devices,
it would hide quietly until it found us.
Despite insufficent postage
and unintelligible handwriting,
you flower toward me.
You are at the door, in the window
knocking on the glass for me to remove the pane,
we, who dissolve like wafers on your tongue.
You shake loose a long braid of love.
I stand on my toes. I squint and look
around for someone else. I point to me.
You mean me. For me. Not me. Never me.

Dinner Party

if I told you that as soon as
I mentioned Ray Carver
you interrupted me
and went on about

knowing him. he and his daughter
stayed with you in Washington.
he was a fine writer. Tess
was not in the picture yet.

how sad about him, you said. when I wanted
to say you interrupted me from saying
that I am always reading the wrong
book, Carver's picture on the back of one.

he looked like an uncle
who tried to undress me
when I was 14 and baby sitting
somewhere in Manhattan

when his wife was pregnant
with their second child.
when he stopped back the second night,
I pretended to be asleep,

using safety pins to fasten
my nightgown shut. he sat on a chair
in the small guest room and watched me
for a long time,

his hands pressed together.
a hair caught under the glass
scars his photo
hanging in my mother's bedroom

to remember her brother
where I forget forgetting that
when I told her, she only said that
she was sure he'd find his way.
but if I told you that

you would have stopped talking to me,
put me instead at the other end of the
table where the Turkish girl was
sitting with the Egyptian Jew from Harvard.

Garden with an L

It must have been quite the thing at the time,
to laminate the front pages of *The New York Times*.
His daughter found the box. The headlines read:
the Invasion of Poland, Crystal Night, the Blitz, D-Day.

She has seen in all this his natty-smooth presence,
a snapshot of him on horseback,
in tennis whites that turned inventors
into business men with crates
and their company name. Only one is left.

Shopkeepers never left their work unfinished.
Those nights he sat late at his table,
shifting his glasses to his forehead
for the serious work, numbers mostly.

So deserted by the friends he brought
to America, he sat darker, more curious,
rubbing his elbows dry and inflamed,
picking his eyebrows until
they were reduced to stubble,
winding rubber bands on his wrists
for sorting, packing.

His daughter believed in *Glarden*,
accepted it as blood and breath. Which,
when asked, she spelled quite simply.
She never thought it strange, a word
no one else owned, as she did the mole
raised high and fearsome on his cheek.
He made the name up, took it
in all its peculiar irrelevance.

And when he died, his daughter gave it up,
folded and tucked it further and further away
until there was no room for it on the invitation,
until all she was allowed to carry with her
was his initial.

pantomime

I stay on the path. He cuts through.
He has done this before. I know

the footprints that dissolve beneath me
when a change is about to come

to the pines taller and wilder
than an accident of opportunity.

No one believes that woods make me
do things I wouldn't ordinarily do.

For a moment I think I am someone else
in a place that either loved my kind or

loathed my kind. Whatever grows here
has gone without water for a long time.

What makes him greedy when it is I
who wants to know who will smile first?

Who will glance out of the corners of their eyes?
And how shall I arrive: from cliffs,

a Dover too familiar to fascinate,
by horseback or boat where a lighthouse draws me

back from the edge, from a place
whose people would otherwise succumb

to the slow thunder beneath them? Steam
rises through the grates in the street.

I know the hairs
in my comb are not mine.

I trace them to a quiet woman who works
all day for one fragile moment tonight.

I unswirl my hair,
lay out my words like a negligee.

Life is not over inside me
not then, not now.

The sound of traffic does not reach us.
Like the earth, memory

spins into my wedding ring.
It glides off my finger

that swells in summer, that
shrinks in winter, only here, only here.

something that shifts

for Bill Heyen

I didn't tell you I don't care much
   for farms and roads, spit ponds.
I don't care much about willows or the lonely
   gray bark of life somewhere
out in the fields.

Today I will not say what I think.
   I will dismount the right man,
confess the mistake and turn my back on myself,
   give my house up to someone else,
shrug and turn away.
   Somewhere I will hear voices and have to go in.

everything finds me here

this is a safe house.
you can find your way from the front
to the back,
which way to go, the least protected
or the one well lit and clean,
the raw feels.

just the same, people worry at thresholds.
they wander from room to room
looking for a place to sleep.
they can put their bare feet down confident
in the brick or white porcelain,
different only in the nature of the clay.

today I don't know who you are.
you enter several doors at once,
each a violation of privacy.

there is a point between us
where everything stops,
wind and warriors.
no diversion or obligations distract.
no noise drops between us to protect me.
nothing stands between us and the terror of
secrets you think I don't know.

whatever occurs when you enter here,
you will not find it empty.

how can I say you are safe here?
I serve you all the safe words
of housework, school, maybe my children
rising somewhere pink and busy,
always busy, so I do not know who stalks them,
degenerate, like a man in a hallway who once
put his hand between my legs.

Chicago in Black and White

1

You were looking for a sandwich.
Everything was shut down.
Some guy in the hotel told you
about a leftover about to
disappear into
the cracks of the alley
under the El where the street lights
are shot and the walls char like despair,
where the owner is white,
the waitress is white,
the prices are white.
It was the kind of place
you wouldn't go hungry.
You didn't look in the eye.
You wouldn't bother counting your change.

You scan the faces like the dial of a radio.
So long as there are lights you are safe.

You ask Andy how it feels tasting pepper with
all that salt.
He said, you get used to it after a while.
We live in two worlds, he said.
Everywhere we go,
we open a white door,
attend a white meeting,
sit on a white toilet,
eat in a white diner.

You enter this street, that train, this shop,
but you do not understand why
there are only two Blacks.
You understand it
in Walnut Creek or Sweet Valley,
but you do not understand it in Toronto
or St. Paul where they mix it up better.
And you do not understand it on your block.

2

Andy said, you don't go to the right places.
You read aloud too well. You perform too well.
Words flat on the page
have to breathe on their own,
without tubes, without speech.

Not like the baby whose legs you patterned
back in the 60s. She lay on a kitchen table
and every day you held her ankles
and walked her legs, as if feeding
a stem would save its sway.

The news reports two children
walked roofs to
create a kingdom by looking up.
They fall off where Curly the transvestite
was killed behind the diner. Are trees
stronger for having their branches broken?
Is twine uncoiled for its threads?

How it takes courage or stupidity to
carouse with people you don't know,
slip on the ice, the sheerest glaze you don't see.
Conversation. You can't anticipate
those whose language you don't speak,
the way it will go.
How someone knows you well enough
to know your nickname and use it gracefully.

Take a year, Andy said. Work isolated from whites.
Be a cripple. How people avoid you.
You get bolder. You go over to people.
Ask questions. Voice opinions.

This is no place for people
to die quietly in their beds.

3

I've made my decision.
I don't want to be just a gardener,
a domestic, a Georgian, a daughter
of everlasting.

Today I am greed. An historian, a prophet,
the blues, the sleaze, shuffling
with Princess Raja,
hustling with Ling-Ling,
wearing a pin stripe suit
and packing a pearl-handled gun.

Today I am swollen with
Ntozaki Shange and Quincy Troupe.
I want to press so hard I fingerprint stone.
I want my Mahalia mouthy,
my hips to frizz like Piaf or Baker
who offends with her skin.
I defend with mine.
I didn't mean to be white.
Most times I'm not.

Tonight my stomach rumbles as if
I am carrying their babies,
their push-ups against my ribs,
their ribs floating into my throat,
their throat into my headbones.

I flex my joints, point my elbows,
thrust my hips into the ground.
Let the cymbals resonate,
sing into my spine,
dreadlocks to armpits,
and the wrap-rip-rap telling
me more than the champagne just opened.
I've doubled in size and opened the valves.
I want to matter. I want to matter.

Listen, Father

1 Photogray

My father was not a pencil drawing
or watercolor. Oils, that's what he was,
that made us seem wealthy and drunk.
He wore a smoking jacket
but never wobbled with love.
His tea was poured only
in a straight-sided glass.
I find them in the shops in Tblisi.

I never saw my father as a man.
I am brave to say that. I am not sure
what I saw him as. It only matters that
he was driven as fingers against
a cut to stop bleeding. He was a Russia into
which we were allowed no entry.

I hear him walking
like a chair dragged across the floor.
He starts with a click, then
taps a chain-like chord.
With circadian regularity it seems to come
now that I myself am closer
to surrender than I was then.

2 Chia

His was simply a glass that withstood
temperature and time,
yet so thin
my lips could touch through it.

When he held a sugar cube in his mouth,
when he rinsed dinner with tea,
mahogany and clear,

his sip was as close as we come to knowing
the earthly thaw that sculpted lakes,
to the thrashing of people into
the ravine, the mass grave at Babi Yar.
A small cemetery rises next to it.

I am blown across Europe and
settle deeply into the country
I once learned about.
Iron, zinc, and coal.
I never believed minerals until now,
the 20 million who died.
I throw salt behind me
to remember them.

Now I do not know where I am stepping,
where the stories are. I bend down,
feel beneath the soil for something familiar,
my father, my mother, a history I might touch.

3 Listen, Father

He is starting to say goodbye.
He already sleeps like the ebb of a tree.
His blanket makes only snatches of sense before
it slips off him. Liver spots boil on his hands.

Somewhere the world and he begin to part.
Silence is something he does not question,
like the coat he holds on to and
wraps around him as if
its weave could keep winter away.
These are difficult things
that I do not talk about though
I have written about them long before my time.

Listen, father with one leg, do not worry.
In other rooms there is walking but no movement.
Music exists but it is better in memory.
These are lessons artists tell their models
from sketch to painting to frame.
Listeners know when poets read their last line.

Circling as Moths Do

I prepare the table. I tie
the pale wool kerchief around my head
and open my palms to the candles
to coax its light,
to see my daily face as I see our earthly walls,
scabbed and broken, better only than
brown grass that survives without care.
Age gnarls that way through
the length of the light,
as long as it lasts and wherever it travels,
the different intensities arriving at my eyes.
I speed up the beating of my wings
and fly toward the light,
            circling as moths do.

We are expected to do this utterly ourselves
in a voice, mouldering.
We feel so lonely in the world that
we come to expect neighbors to talk
            in a foreign tongue.

I am trying to understand you among
your things,
in your closet or drawer, in the shed,
the attic box.
I do not tell you that you have made a mistake.
You have wandered into the wrong woman.
You have not gotten me gifts.
You have reminded me of the flaws
            in my body.

Everything about loving is strange.
I knew earlier than most.
My face no longer obeys.
Better to step away;
leave it rotting on the side,
the mice droppings that find it at night
            in corners without candles.

Most of all

We could write poems that no one
would understand.
We would keep them in a drawer,
send them to special people who
privilege mysterious things:
a turn of phrase, a line break here or there.
The peculiar lack of restraint we would enjoy
in moments of great complexity,
speculations away from things,
a leaf, an empty doorway.
Nothing nearly as lawful as a spider's web,
nothing nearly as useful as the ribs of a leaf.

We make love to something we toss off as
terminal punctuation.
We leave bits and pieces lying around
so we can return
at some reckless moment to claim them.

We are never sure we are talking
to people who love us.
The selfishness of not remembering
who they are. Our children, our friends
try to make the best of it.

We sketch the scenes so
when we think, we will think evenly,
fit around trees like the sun,
and people will be drawn to us.

In a wilderness of our own making
we do not hear but nod as if we do.
We look at their family photos,
smile and pretend to fathom the relationships.
As we leave, we catch a glimpse of ourselves,
wide-eyed, knowing to blend like owls to winter.

Affairs of Sight

I am surrounded by row houses
on a small street just north
of an undisputed middle,
without parking,
intersections, or driveways,
a wrought iron city of numbers.

I look out on a liquid sky to pear trees,
a fishing net, a rowboat or two,
to berries that soften and spoil,
the merest graying at the banks of the canal.
That this faded sleeve once replaced
a road that now smirks back at it.

I did not know how to find my way to the locks,
the square black knife poised to
chop up the water so helpless and forgiving,
or to the clumps of trees like army trucks
that someday they will find.
I never looked for the canal or questioned it.
I never saw it on a map. I never believed it
or considered the elderberries along the path.
I hold one between my teeth
and pluck off the leaves, just for the moment.

How long must I wait till I can call this scene mine?
How long must I stay: watch, grasp, and study it,
as squatters who outlive the landlord but
never come to own?

Clouds are shot from the tank they
try to put me in, the eyelids they try to
close over me, the touch
they try to take out of my view.

I defy anyone to summarize me.
The harbor, I built it, put curtains up,
made the beds, know when it's tired or sick.
I dare anyone to say I cannot claim the Erie,
Panama, or Corinth from the moment my eyes
gather them in all their urgencies. The Suez,
the Gulf of Aqaba. And I will own more—
Piraeus at dawn, Gibraltar begotten
above my feet—wait and see.

Once I bridge my grit to slide,
squeeze my ribs between ridge and cleft,
the steep earthly climbs,
once I stake my claim with iridescent strips,
pour the cement, set the orange girders between,
penetrate the geometry for one pure moment.
That my eyes alone could wear away
the foot of Michaelangelo's David.

For a Moment I am Not a Stranger

I know everyone. Walking is easy.
I ignore them. It is trivial.
It is comfortable
like a tissue in my pocket.
It feels warm for one moment
because there is no dust or dried mud.
I have been there every day
and my presence divides evenly between
my nostrils and tongue. I can breathe.
I do not overhear conversations
nearby. I don't need permission
for what to say next,
no more sounds from someone
feeling uncomfortable and frightened.
I know that nakedness is no longer
fitting for children in public.
Tea and apples finally go together.

photojournalism

the doctor spends 10 minutes with you
the doctor spends 1 minute with you
the doctor is in surgery
the doctor is on rounds
the doctor is gone for the day
the doctor is away for two weeks
the physician's assistant is the doctor
the nurse is the doctor
the aide is the doctor
housekeeping takes your pulse
transporters keep your pulse
the answering service checks your meds
the residents change their sex,
their voice, their tilt
the social worker writes the script
the interns translate the script
the pharmacist delays the script
they slide in, they slip away, glide away
the person you trusted your body to
flattens into a white ribbon
that thins and melts,
that eyes the exit,
a finale, empty and slant from the door
words, sliced in half by its frame
words, whose hands are on the door knob,
that volunteer no information,
that answer in short spurts,
like the faucet of the sink
you spit into
the doctor hedges like a bet
he takes motion out of your legs
your hands curl around them

Eclipse

the sun is leaving Istanbul today at 2:30
for Rhodes or anywhere. we pound for time
and flesh to center us, our energies.
it has been long in coming,
given the distractions,
the 2 women on the corner
trying to be Western. the one
with a red and yellow look
marks her prey,
an idle sort of man
walking somewhere
on the heat of the day,
like so many
wherever that world is,
as does the day advance more or less
if he is hopelessly innocent
and seems to know where
he is going.
so little gets done from dawn to dusk
despite his resolve.
everything is measured
from him when time collapses
into us or the bystanders.
we can never be sure about them,
the janitors, off to the side,
the smoking gladiolas,
not misunderstanding.
they do not make it better
but they do not stand in her way.
I don't know if she got
her man in the end.
he was startled no doubt,
her being white and stringy,
her bra strap showing.

the privilege of form

The world theorized the circle,
the perfection of things embraced,
their eternal return.
Coliseums copied the celestial order
monks moralized its beauty.
The moon was sliced into bindis
that celebrated the human face.

Rulers settled into palaces
and came to climb the circular stairs,
a reminder of the privilege of form.
Virtue came to terms with utility.
The best thing about wheels was that they rolled.

Water is circular, the well from which it springs,
bubbles and drops, balanced and symmetrical.
The circle is closed, definitive, strong,
never backing people into a corner or
forcing them against the ropes.
When everything barricades, circles protect.

They shed to rings, pills, dots, births
lush with fluid. Tunnels are round,
red is round, its fetus warm without end.
While cities edge off into tumbleweed and rot,
the circle cleanses. Flowers open.
Nothing is unwilling to be born.

Echoes like smoke rings boast one,
after another, after another,
past our cheeks, past our arms and ovals,
millions of voices revolving
on crystalline spheres,
the seasons and their fruits.
Even canopied by sky,
the sun and stars surround,
dancers in orbit, the spread of light.
Ballet is round, song is round, all join hands
or merely two.

to the body at calm

if they didn't die of typhoid
if they didn't die in childbirth
if they didn't stiffen from frostbite
or decay from jungle heat
if they weren't drowned in floods
if they didn't cramp from dysentery
or choke from pneumonia
or suffocate in sandstorms
leaning into the night like remorse,

they ruptured their backs
they were crushed by stone, snapped in half
paralyzed by lifting, dragging
block after block for the marble ship
locked in the lake, to the cathedral doors,
to the Great and Wailing Walls.
they lost their balance climbing bamboo
scaffolding or descending on it

how many would tear just in the climb,
just in the carving of a frieze,
designing a cherub, etching milky ceremonial
ceilings and painting them with gold leaf,
the dizziness that comes from looking up
when everything else falls away
and you are unprotected from the belief
in the value of great things except

human life, abundant and trivial.
it is not meant to last. it doesn't have to.
there are always another 1000
to whip along with the obelisk, pink and glossy.
the guide says that what makes it remarkable
is that it was carved from
one unblemished piece of granite.
just when the earth closed over 10 million,
Africans became slaves
quarried and lashed together.

I remember pictures of coal miners
interred with the stones that still
warm their families. the mourning period
lasts no more than a pulse,
but for the infinitesimal
moment that I am today here.

That's how it happens

to Caroline whose eyes scatter me with shadows.
I soothe her hair oiled and segregated
and dare talk
about goodness and hope when

her rent is 13 dollars a month
in the Delmar Loop. Where you lock your car,
barbwire your garden, carry no money.

Where they chop off your clothes line,
cut into your porch, dig up your back yard,
steal your sidewalk for the new road.
I borrow her mouth and

blow breath into
this singed and moody Ghana,
who tests all waters, who never speaks first,
whose smile comes late or not at all.

Isadora Duncan would know

1

I explain it this way:
You are naked. You have nothing
around you but soil and sky,
not a mound to stand on, not a bean or pit
or sound collecting in the brush, but
what your voice pushes out and falls
to a limpid arpeggio.

You are within yourself
the breadth of your scalp
the sharp of your skin
a mind with only hands.

Your lips, the shudder of your elbow,
what tightens, browns, and peels,
disqualifies you for anything more
than thought and reach.

There is little you do
but propel your legs up,
stretch your head into the air,
strike out against the ocean with the
soles of your feet, grow your hair
into a storm then untangle it as rain.

You dig but only with your nails
and toe bones.
You throw but only with arms shackled
to your shoulders.
You have ten fingers
outraged against the night.
Four limbs only scratch against stone.
You cannot smooth it with your cheek
or warm it with remembrance.
You have steps of only hips and hands
cartwheels, leaps.
Nothing is nearby for you
to sift through and cherish,
just you, nothing more than
knowing a human body can only do so much.

2

Today is one scarf different,
a mere handkerchief.
You approach it charitably,
touch it, inch across its rainbow.
You bracelet your ankle,
tie the hanky around your wrist.
The dervish uncurls the day so far
as a headdress then transports you,

waving arm with scarf,
teeth with scarf, toes and tongue,
your height with it.
How it complicates the drama.
How many curves in time and place,
the straights and droops,
that soft baton between peace and war.

When you do a Thai dance
you know how silk extends knowledge,
reshapes the arcs within you that
you thought you'd never find,
minute inventions in blown glass:
What can be done with breath.

You wear trees for a skirt.
You pull them into you.
They climb like acrobats.
They implicate the horizon.
The human is the moment,
the morning, the prow of a ship.

3

But this is not fast.
What succumbs is slow and methodical,
one branch, then another, then
every shade between,
the intricate forms impossible to believe,
infinite alterations of years you
hold between your fingers, whatever becomes
of your life that dates from
the moment you first bent

and twirled with wide-cuffed sleeves,
as glorious as could be
depended on what you held
between your fingers
or what shriveled for lack thereof.
Imperceptibly it comes to shoes,
taps, heels upon heels, ladders,
to ceilings, to roofs and minarets.
The human is the only city with full ramparts,
walls and gates. Temple bells and timpani,
the whole of cosmic space in a rim of tree,
the imperial self.
The raveling of hand upon hand upon hand
is all the Aswan Dam is,
concrete holding up your hurrah.

Travelling the Human Curve ⎯⎯⎯⎯⎯⎯⎯⎯⎯⎯

meadow stars

And I would save every bill, post card,
receipt in a box in the basement
and expect my beneficiaries
to look at the ticket to Kabuki-za
and thrill that they saw it at my seat
in the high, hot balcony that August day.

Half the sky was propped up by men,
the other half by women subdued at their knees,
sweeping their hands around their hem.
A heavenly powder paled their faces.
Shrill crows and dragons
and morning glories plucked at one another.
Violins plucked. I step over a cadence,
lose my bearings to the Milky Way,
plucking the wheat and corn that night
somewhere near Des Moines. I stopped
the car and held my children up so they
could see the meadow stars, so within reach
they could wear the sky as a scarf.

The shocking clarity of the stalks
through them, the long straight pull
of the bow along the tassels, rice newly bending.

When I taste the simple rice noodle,
the clearest jelly of the night sky,
when I suck and swallow it,
I cannot tell whether I am an adult or child.

What is it in this sight
that makes me forget Asia,
separate it from long thin fields,
furrows so close I cannot walk
between the rice grasses.
The grasses yellow like a ticket
stub, small change, a tissue,
something to hold on to.

The yellow, a loess, is thick and elemental.
There is nothing particularly precious
or final about it,
this delicacy we get in abundance. And
what of the machines that separate us
from our stems, blue
like you are walking on sky
and closer to the country that raised you.

Travelling the Human Curve

The birds are sleek and wooded. The wreaths are dense and as brown
as Russian bread, as the Georgians whose Black Sea stirs into Armenia,
whose cossacks spin to their brides. Their kerchiefs ring Mt. Ararat, and
Noah trails down into hairy Turkish cities that sip tea and pass the time
with halvah pressed oily and abundant from sesame, as sweet as the
Negev is salt, as the Israeli Bedouins who undulate arm in arm to the flute
and wear kepot, caps like the Egyptians of Nubian darkness whose songs
sway across the deserts to the strangers from Morocco all tassled and
tambourine. Their coins clap. Their henna twirls. Their palms curl out.
Their gypsy fingers snap North to the Castilia. The violins and castanets
speed up, who can keep up, with the cordovan and coffee, the courtesies of
the French, their sloe eyes, their vines. Into their mahogany languid hair
are woven grapes of the Rhone. Lausanne, polite and flowered, whose bows
are always wide and glossy and white. How they deepen and disappear into
the Black Forest, beard to mustache, Rhine to Ruhr, solvent to soot, to the
folk dances of the Germans, of the Polish (or are we Soviets) drinking
water from the same glass as the Georgians at the square grey vendors
along Kreshchatik. In Hidro Park there is a ride without a name. It works
like this: Two boys swing in a basket back and forth, harder and harder
until they complete a circle. This is the way it was intended: The music
shapely and perceptible, all the toe shoes pink, the swallows so familiar

Scenes from the Soviet, 1988: Twos

Near Passaneury the rivers Aragvi and Kura
weave brown and white. They say it is the hair
of two sisters who once loved the same man.
Each died so the other could have him.

Now wreaths of linden flow down them
to be picked up by fiancées.

Tonight I lay out my desk for the bride,
for melodies that wait patiently,
that believe in beginnings
and perfect things.

Her cape covers her hands and cannot be
touched until her wedding day.
A vessel in the ground stores the wine.

How rich we would be,
how few words would be written
if everything were right.
The dress made of fresh water pearls,
caviar beading on her bouquet.

In summer the dusk is as transparent as batiste.
People gather near the Dnieper to sing.
A man from the group leads.
We do a circle dance so as
not to desert one world for the other.

Scenes from the Soviet, 1988: pause

I come over
the sheer ledge of the Caucasus
to simpler cities.
I had forgotten how gloriously their
faces shine. Here I touch the stage.
There are no props. Hand gestures
choreograph the curve of earth and place.

In the markets a girl bunches
carrots with their hair. She gives me
cones of paprika and cilantro.
An old woman works at her crates
and picks tomatoes from a pail.
Another carries turnips and beets in her apron.
They eat on the ground.
Nothing gathers so well as a kitchen table.

Scenes from the Soviet, 1988: Posterity along the Arbat

The crowds climb in front
of each other, the longest line
for bananas from Ecuador.
We carry an empty bag, stand on our toes
on the chance that we see something.
A puppet plays the harmonica.
We clap neatly for monkeys
sitting on wind-up cars. We reach in.
Our hands grasp nothing we want.

Street artists draw silhouettes
with crayon and pastel.
Russia is a camera that
cannot take photos of itself,
that cannot leave the country.

If we were left
with one piece of paper,
how quickly could we write on it
and what would we say
before a new generation lined up
to be remembered in a sketch?
And who would save it for posterity?

Artists work long hours
in any weather for us who
do not recognize our profile,
our voice on tape,
who live on myths of meaning.

Functionaries carry
oranges and meat in attaché cases,
as hard as concrete.
Full citizens
get to choose their worlds.
Others take what's handed out.

Red Square fits like a jigsaw puzzle.
We wind and unwind
ourselves at Lenin's tomb.
Conversation is rare.

A street guitarist in cyrillic melody
fights into a song that
fights into the police.
An unmarked car takes him away.
It happens quickly.

Scenes from the Soviet, 1988: the dead zone

I am told not to eat berries or mushrooms,
drink the water, or walk in the rain.
A gray acid film labors over my belly
30 kilometers around.

I dream I am a cripple. My legs are skinny
and limp like rubber bands. People avoid me.

Days drop out of sight.
All things are sealed.
My baby is boarded up.
How do I ask for help?

The plucking season is from May to October,
tea on acid soil. The top 3 leaves make
the best tea. Women make the best pickers.
They do not work in the dust.

Wednesday. It rained at the farm.
The forceps are contaminated.
The milk is irradiated.
The tea plants are trimmed to
grow again and again. The leaves
wither and wind around their spinal cord.

Children and mothers
pregnant or those about to be
are told to leave.
But how far and to where?
This is Kiev and not Chicago.
I have stones in my womb.

Cicadas live 17 years in my cocoon
and come out as mayflies.
My baby is born without a mouth
and dies of starvation within a day.

Things are different inside the hotels.
Food falls from the sky.
They press ashes on my forehead,
Tincture of iodine on the harvest.
I get accustomed to April 26th.

.

Scenes from the Soviet, 1988: Taken a Chance

You would have registered at the police.
I would have ridden black.
You would have worn the arm band.
I would have played dead.
You would have put up your hands.
I would have spread my legs.
You would have rolled up your sleeve.
I would have amputated my numbers.
lied, changed my name,
become a farmer in the south of France,
pressed grapes and
stood in the road with a bolt of lightening.
I would have dug a tunnel under the wall,
flung myself over it, crashed through the barrier.

It was always cloudy around Krakow, hooded like nuns,
girls riding bicycles like nuns.
The heavy odor of oil and fire, the putrid smoke,
it was nothing new.
Table umbrellas close for the season like
alter boys at prayer.
The air is still. The trees shudder.
When the beginning and end come together,
when the garden dies,
the pear, the apple turn to wood and split.

Scenes from the Soviet, 1988: The Night Bar in Kiev

Beyond the doormen, behind the desk,
below sea level,
tourists press around the bars
like gamblers to luck.

Impressionism is served best
on a napkin of anonymity and
a smoky gaze, cheerless laughter.

Guards sift the foreigners
from the natives, the soil from the stones.
An American lets in the local guide.

Victor is not worried that
someone will find him.
He has sneaked in before.
He has done his military duty.
He is married one year at 22.

There are books so Victor can
talk with Ludlum, Fitzgerald,
Hammett, Hemingway. I give him Salinger.
There is beer and vodka.
There are smokes, $10 strong.
I put a pack down on the table.
It talks for me.

The walk through the undergrounds is safe.
There are few beggars. A drunk
slouches next to me on the metro.
He smiles dreamily. His arm supposes
my waist. I smell the sweat
of the women, pulpy and coarse.
The conductor calls out the stops.
I count syllables and stations until mine,

Until I begin to believe these ways
after weeks of searching,
hours beneath the surface.
I am caught in the wires of the radio,
taking things apart, the old alarm clock,
putting them back together.

It is enough that I extend my hand.
I travel deeply into the well.
How long it takes to reach the reason for things
without instruments of navigation,
like cone roofs built without nails.
The lights of the trains blink.
They stall like the smoke
in the night bar from midnight to 5.
There are dead spots on the tracks.

Bars make me sudden and simple.
Circles swell under my eyes.
Hair grows out of my chin.
Russians still give up their
seats for old people. Which
limb of my body feels this?

The floor lady keeps the keys to 1000 rooms
24 hours of every day and every night.
The mother of wine and the sword
is a country whose cheeks
crease from restless sleep.
The foreigners, loud and misunderstood,
give her their room card.
She gives them their keys.
The doors of their rooms close
and I do not know them anymore.

Scenes from the Soviet, 1988: A Full Frontal Shot

And eyes beveled calm trying to catch the color
    of my gods, the cross hairs of my trip.
Glass separates us and protects him.
He stencils my height on the mirror behind me.
He traps my neck and shoulders, the top of my head.
He speaks like a stapler.
They are busy.
I tell them I am not a business.
I am not a poet.
I wear no tinted glasses.
I am matte finished.
They are not busy.
They search my bag. They find pictures, notes.
They chisel through its pages.
I have receipts for amber but not for caviar.
I have a litre of pepper vodka, 200 smokes.
I declare my children, a bangle of freedom,
    and other gemstones.
I carry no Bible, no sensitive books.
I take out no Jews.
I bring none in.
The customs officer stamps my arrival and departure.
I guard my visa. Still, its seals and signatures
    disappear like nested dolls.
A man squeezes into my hand the address
    of someone in Israel.

Scenes from the Soviet, 1988: Intourist

Small as Latvia, she squints,
even in places unlit by the sun.
There is no sign that
anyone has been here before.

This is more apparent than real,
she says. Soviets travel.
We have resorts and sunbathing.
We have cakes, chocolates.
We have tampons.

Once I could have answered with
Leningrad, where beauty
lies in its palaces, its canals,
its silver money penny.

What stays with me is her voice,
so hard I cannot make footprints
even in fresh snow.
This is not what I had in mind,
I answer.

Yesterday she repeated the tour book,
czar for czar.
Her mouth pinched like a paper clip.
Her sentences were deaf at both ends.
We do not want to visit
the states, she said,
We have our life, our country.
Americans ask too many questions.
Put a poem to that if you can.

Scenes from the Soviet, 1988: Wheat and Wide Boulevards

Russia is a road crew in green
deep gray, breathing like a
smoke stack.

No one bends over Russia and
helps her on with her shoes.

Russia holds a rod and wears
a cap.

No one steadies her walk.

The lank leather face of labor,
the feel of fist.

She is barley soup with
a mutton bone in it.

His sleeves are rolled up and
tight around his ripe,
waxy arms.

Modesty deserts her.

The Kremlin bulges,
his neck and shoulders bulge,
the hanky in his back pocket.

Her breasts lay loose and flat
on her stomach, like anemic infants.

We bring Russia books every
day. He wants to read about the
bicycle, the kind he used to ride.

Her pelvis spans the Black to
Japan Sea, a country so vast I
am unable to embrace her, let
alone be her student.

He remembers climbing on the
roof to roll the leaves of the
cherry tree into cigarettes.

She takes rivers into her mouth,
holds for a moment, then sprays
her clothes for ironing.

He still seals the cracks in his
fingers from the cold
with clear cement.

There is dirt under her nails.

He looks at me, at what I am writing,
then dozes off.

The sores on old people do not heal.

Scenes from the Soviet, 1988: Slight Attention to Problems that have No Name

We are equal
      except for the $7 tickets the
      Soviets buy for 2.
We are innocent except for the waitress who
      hides a nested doll under a napkin.
      I put it in my bag.
We are safe
      except for the side mirror broken
      off our car during the night.
We are free
      but not to leave.

The true subject of progress
      travels by wind and water not by
industrial pipes and exit permits,
      with no money left to resole its shoes.

This country thickens me,
      electrifies the fence along my mouth.
It cools its fingers in the Black Sea.
      I am thrown against its callouses.
The wound lies helplessly like a grave.

Scenes from the Soviet, 1988: view of Gorky Park after rain

The sun finally arrives in vanilla-wide bows and Nina.
I take her picture. She refuses my stick of gum. She sucks
the end of her braid while a woman in green waits for
the bride in white cotton and lace who crosses Krymskij
Val between the cars with a serene lack of self-
consciousness, having just bought her veil at Riga market from
a girl whose mother sells currants at the metro where trams
bring people to stores at which they can buy nothing.

Moon and Breeze Festival

I have wanted to return
to the city of lucky money.
Here I smile with shaved hair
and gold teeth. People
take pictures of me and clap.
I wave and they translate it.

The food from Shanghai is thick and red and strong.
A carpenter sleeps among his shavings. His door
is open to an inner order I want to grasp.
I hear it breathe even when the gypsies
cry hello, hello: Jade, pearls, silk, beads,
to buy, to buy, anything you want.
Crows eat at my hair.
I wear loose black slacks
gathered at the waist and ankle.

It drizzles in the park. I open
my umbrella onto a low branch of a tree
and start my lesson beneath.
I am the one among. I am a garden
that visitors leave every evening.
I face away from crowds
so as to enter the peace I seek.

Many people enter the laws of Tai Chi,
but only those with money go out.
They tell me I can trade locations, but I
cannot move quickly or freely.

I ask you to think of me when we were young
and open like petals.
I still boil them into soup.
I still press snake into wine and
pound insects into powder.

This is what they have taught me.
How do we come to ourselves if not by learning,
and send it falling from the sky to save people,
missing each other by only a thread.

sorrow and the range of light

People are leaving
messages everywhere, on my walls,
at my feet, in my ears and mouth.
Fortune paper is waiting for messages
to send to you and to me.

Messages hang like Spanish moss.
They are after me.
They tell me things are all right
even though you are far away or I am.

One million paper cranes
shroud the statues at Hiroshima,
a sign of luck and long life, but
somewhere else. Their colors
are naive and brave, folded
with geometric directness, so that

if we lifted them
as kites, they would swoon across the sun
in its blinking closeness,
the one mortal moment, protective
like Buddha's extra arms that float around us

then fall into chains dragged ferociously over us
buried by sheer weight. To be silent is to be wise.

The streets are not silent or wise.
War comes, bows down, and woos me.
I know something is wrong and try to fight it.

People are waiting inside my words to show me
the way to your home. A spirit returns
and I find him at the train station
in the small shops, on your street. He remembers
you from the time you knew everyone so well
they didn't look the same, though
you never said it.

The temple bells bring words, announce
them with a lantern.
At the door is a small wall
that bad luck stumbles over.
Someone is going to take something.
I do not leave the door open,
but I can't move fast enough.

Rice paper is designed
like the inside of a coconut,
textured, meaty, and sweet.
The future blesses the threshold or
the trunk of a tree to which the paper is tied.

Bad fortune leaves its shadow
on the land. Somewhere in wartime
a parent is always crying.

People fan themselves with incense.
they cup the wishing water with their hands,
swallow it. Its tide levels them in their palms,
written on one side, waiting on the other.

They throw money into the magic water,
into coffins with slats,
the slats of mulberry bark they write wishes on.
They slip coins in the folds of Buddha's robe.
Messages are stuffed into my pleats.
Poems are slipped beneath my wallpaper.

The note in a bottle is adrift
on a sea of streets where
I wait for you to send word my way.

The planes get louder and more menacing.
The whole world floats down in a word,
but still no one speaks.
Come out of your wall,
open your folds,
unwrap the message,
say what you mean.

Sun Spots from the Soft Seat Waiting Room

Among a quartet of mountains
China squats at the flower and bird market.

The melon rind, the lotus, seed and root
are tender and edible. Nothing is wasted.
Farmers sway not with baskets but with
carrying poles that bring baskets along
a road once made of ice,
a golden river that carried rock,
that protected crops from fire.

From a watchtower the only thing
I see with the naked eye
is the Great Wall. Consider walls.
No culture is without them,
the side of them that is meant.
Some people seal their walls, not trusting
their bodies in the normal way.
Others plant notes in the Wailing Wall,
sallow like prayers at Execution Wall,
a small wall at Auschwitz,
maybe fourteen feet long.

The Poles do not welcome us into Warsaw.
In the ghetto cemetery
headstones slant but do not fall.
Prayers are held down by stones.
It rains and the words dissolve,
but the paper hardens into mortar
that speaks by sheer persistence.

Laborers at lunch walk along the paths,
point and sneer and urinate in my face.
I leave the city with stain
on my lips but they will stain even more
because tomorrow I go to Auschwitz
where I see 514 pieces of children's clothes.

I ask everyone I can find:
Who would wear the dress
of a dead Jewish child,
shoes, ribbon found
in the membranes of Execution Wall—
those for whom execution was too good,
death was too easy.
I ask everyone I can find:
Who today could live in a town with
such an address, 137 Ulica, Oświęcim,
Auschwitz, even though in Grinzing
I see an old Nazi with the naked eye.

Breaking the Fast

The second time my father died
we were cleaning up his things
and went through his books.

In my dream he reads in Russian
and I understand.
I send him my books and care about
receiving his. It is medieval times.
Across Europe I read for
answers from stained glass windows.
Words fall from poplars, pile up,
and burn. I barely speak.

It is hard to believe I am in Warsaw.
But it is not hard to believe Warsaw
is in Poland: Life does not stand straight here,
with its cold sores and split lips.
The grit, we taste it. The gravel thrown
down keeps our memory from slipping.

I'm trying to find my father
all over in my station. I look in my eyes.
I am in a box car. I am a box car.
The tracks hiss through me to the cemetery.

The business card of the caretaker
gives the name: Pincus's son,
an odd way to mean oneself.
But there is a certain logic to it
since we never knew him better
than the moment we hunted him down
and ate at his gate,
his mouth musty as Yom Kippur.

Passers-by remember the old man.
They stare and jeer without a trace.
But they do not go unnoticed.
I stand my truth. I have my way.

No more spitting on the footstones,
laughing at the strange writing.
No more numbers.
Now, my name. I write it
in all my father's books.

The India Series: Confusion Planting

1

This is what you do. When beggars approach,
stop, step back, and circle behind them.
They will understand and leave you alone.

Do not talk to strangers. Do not answer them.
Do not meet their eyes. Do not smile or
acknowledge them. They will not harm,
but they will mistake it for encouragement
and follow you home.

Do not accept anything handed you
by someone you don't know.
Do not wear your silver heavily
in your nose or on your ankles lest
you be mistaken for rich.

Beware of men who keep coins in their ear.
Peddlers. Close your eyes and wave them away.

Watch your bag. If you sleep on the train,
use it as a pillow.
Do not let anyone carry it,
especially in the Delhi station.

Do not trust men with spaces between
their teeth.
Ask directions only of security police
or of natives wearing white shirts
and carrying portfolios. They speak English
and will not mislead you.

Keep your eyes straight as if you are
carrying pots of fire on your head.
Keep them down for the goat dung.

I have bought you new sandals.
When you take them off at a shrine,
put them in your bag and carry them with you.

Do not take your eyes off the Taj.
Do not listen when the guards
tell you to leave.
Watch it at dusk and during the full moon.
Watch it at dawn. The rickshaw will wait for you.

2

Your money. Do not give more
than you owe.
You will not get change.

Small notes are without value if
they are missing corners or
torn at the crease.
Use them for tipping.
See stamps cancelled in front of you.

Do not stop to finger the silks
hanging outside the stalls.
Do not eye them or enjoy them.
Say no the first time and walk away.

Look at shop windows only
when the shops are closed.
There is no room for indecision.
Make up your mind.
Do not look helpless or lost.
Decide alone.

Examine the stitching on shawls.
Is it even or ravelling?
Examine the design.

Is it stamped or hand painted?
Feel the weight of the silk.
Put one end in your mouth
as you walk to keep it from falling.

Do not eat samosas on the street,
sip the sweet lime drink
or the juice of the sugar cane.
Oil your hands before
you drink the milk of the jack fruit.
Eat the first slice
of watermelon before flies settle on it.

Touch food only with your right hand.
Use only your finger tips to hold
your bread for scooping up the curries.
Before you taste aniseed, sift it
through your fingers until it runs clean.

Eat street food straight from the fire,
but do not let hunger crawl between
your legs. You will be viewed with scorn
and no respectable man will have you.

3

You will marry a man whose fingers
fit into the handle of a cup.
He will go with you to pick sari silk.

Your father will wear a pink turban
at your wedding. You will sit on
a platform with your husband and smile.

Learn to tell raw silk from gauze.
Learn the difference between
thatch stuffed into tea cozys and
paper stuffed into vests. You will
appreciate the bed of life.

Keep your head covered.
Do not think about your hair.
No matter how you fix it,
your face will not change.
Braid your hair into bamboo from which
your home will be made.

Remember to show respect.
This is how *namaste* is done.
Place your palms together and
hold them upward as in prayer,
lower your eyes, and bow slightly.

Tie a string to the Taj grillwork
and make a wish.
Keep ashes away from your mouth.
Wear a tassel of jasmine every day.
No matter how much you pay the taxi wallah,
it is never enough. Watch that
gold thread does not turn into string.

The India Series: The Turbulent Mirror at a Shrine called Jagdish

We all have cancer on our tongues,
our death songs, our mother songs,
our travel songs, white satin bows
or tainted childhoods.
Identity, crisis, resignation.
I pad around in those rooms too,
and they winter over in my garage.
When I have travelled far enough,
I come to Udaipur, the lake giving me
a chance to see myself twice.

I ring the bell. I touch my forehead,
rub holy water on it, wax my head and hair.
I offer gram flour and *ghee*, palm leaves,
paper, money. Above all, give money.

In the morning I am sorry for not
writing down the words that
make me twitch with surprise,
the delicacy of my home at 7 am.
My parents were awake but their voices
were limp and sweet as lovers tend
to be afterward.

I believed important decisions
were made then.
Things were solved like at no other time.
Everything was fascinating and possible.

I take an offering from the alter and
give it to chalky brown children who only
resemble their parents after I understand
the days and nights of their eyes.

If I could do it again, I would
learn from broken bottles,
the front door kicked in.
She stood naked in front of the house,
beaten with a stick. The police came.

There are craters in our thoughts,
deep highways where the cold mist collects.
I weave across the dotted line,
steer around animals as indifferent as rock.
A hill is near, but the road up it is long
with exits when we know we are in for the night.

The India Series: Bombay, Between the Unbreathing

A grash brown stain
of a man squirms on the
pavement like a sick pigeon.
His head is forced
to one side as
if lodged in a brace.
One leg twists under itself.
the other,
its thigh ends in a point.

One wing spreads flat and still.
The other flails to escape itself,
making circle waves and
churning him
into a small puddle where
he pauses to sip and cool,
head dipped low as in a curtsy.

An oil cloth for coins
is spread next to him. Who lays
it out and
collects the change. Who feeds
him, his ancient fig roots. And
when the dust storm blots
his sweat, shackles him
against the pavement, and
rounds his spindled limbs
till he vanishes,
who brushes the sand
from his eyelids. Who sucks
it from his throat.
Who carries him till the
wind slackens.
The tour goes on and
we are sorry, only one bag
permitted on the plane.

The India Series: Reverse Winds and the First Spice

1

for weeks Calcutta is sluggish
from sleeping under a bus,
living in a pipe, pissing to a wall,
washing with soap on the stoops,
all day long throwing water on the streets,

all day long nothing but dirt
coughs back and forth.
we live in branches of a system built
to let rainwater drain from its mouth,
storm sewers large
enough for people to stand upright,
pipe dwellers whose deformities go unnoticed,
like dogs rigid as rain clouds and abandoned
along the marshy outlets of creeks.

every year the marshes are separated by rope.
salt water is agitated into pans
until it is sucked into a greedy sun.
grains of us crystallize.
we are raked into pyramids.

fishnet protects the unsold when the rain is
unseasonal. lepers, cripples, the blind and
malnourished are the first unit of exchange.

2

this year the *El Niño* wreaks havoc
on the world: storms
vandalize the coasts of California,
Peru, Ecuador.
there is drought in Australia.
Indonesia drifts East
with the sift and winnow,
rod and string puppets, the drama
of sticks and tarpaper children.
an overhead lamp sends their
shadows onto a white cotton sky.
the ragged red sand cannot hold us
from evaporating.

people trying to find water clog the sewers,
so scarce it is, so bent toward forests
are the fires of Borneo. the stench of exhaust,
soot, smoke rises. the soil gets sick.

it collects under our nails and between our toes.
it seeps into our fields, infests the grasses,
chokes our very seeds. springs into
the very bread of our body,
our farms are dying. now our water
is burning. people rot. tropical rainfall spreads.

we place wafers on our tongues,
ashes on our foreheads, sip defective beer.
grains of us, the taste of cleft and
brine is served on our plate.

monsoon clouds bring joy till
children are lashed by them,
they scatter like gravel.
they melt into the earth or drown.

3

when the winds come they remind me
of what temporary means for
the childhood of India.
it is, as someone once said, a sky of orphans
in a city of corpses when
there is a collision between ocean
and atmosphere. the anger must go
somewhere. 900 million droplets
flow disinherited. the rapids
are called violent by some.
the banks hemming them in are
called violent by no one.

El Niño is a broom without a stick.
a fiber brush keeps the dry season from
overtaking us. unthatched, we are
soggy and lifeless. our lips
are not allowed to touch the communal
faucet of the sea, which,
like salt in rain, we all return to.

The India Series: Today I am standing in
the middle of a postcard

1

on which the women string flowers and
the men wear them.
In the *chowk*: jute sacs sand twine
shaved heads rope burlap bamboo
hemp reed pigeon peas mung beans
lentils barley corn cinderblocks ashes
nut cutters, foot scrubbers, barbers,
lime and betel containers,
vermilion bottles, money boxes
crimsonmagentaorangeyellow tinsel,
women carrying pots wood food incense.
One pushs a cart that carries bricks.
Her baby swings, cradled between its wheels.

Jan Path, street of the people, has raven
poor in its eyes. Blood from betel
nuts spits on the cities.
The sky purples where a rain of *bindis*
weeps on dirt bricks.
The lips of the Ganges close and
swallow its victims. Sand drifts over
me until I am covered and
my country disappears. I don't see stars.

In the India of my dreams women wear a red
so brilliant they set fire to disease.
From the India of my dreams rises
bright sweet water for wisdom
and health and prosperity. In my dreams
I view the Taj during the full moon.
The mosques are not looted.

2

Women are silent like a secret.
I hide behind *jharokha*, an arched
window balcony. I see outside
but I am not myself seen.
I arrange my scarves away
from the tension of my belly and
the heat of my thighs. Nothing
but desire curls around my waist.
I wait on the women's line to buy
tickets. I ride the women's train.

In the India of my dreams blood comes
from the only natural exit inside me.
In the India of my dreams I settle
into my body and its sensations.
I make silky gestures and geometric
movements. I discover my breasts and
know what lips and neck are for.
In my dreams I stand on any line.

3

In India no one changes his earthen body.
I cannot grow into light skin like children
into hand-me downs. My place springs
from the mouth, arms, and thighs of Brahma
and cannot be altered. I see myself,
one hand grown larger than the other.

In the India of my dreams the new moon
is wiser than the full moon which
chooses the past and is always
dying. The new moon promises, always promises.
In the India of my dreams I defend
with the shine of my skin. I teach
the wealth of my spirit. In my dreams
I grow like wild flowers into date palms.

Things Women ——————————————————————

elasticity

depending on lipstick as I can't my
drooping cheeks, my lips and neck,
the bags beneath my eyes, what's
missing, what's gone, my barrette,
my earring, what spots my glasses,
what's stuck on my chin, what fits,
what's out of place, what's swollen,
what's moist on my forehead, what
shows, what's chapped, what's blotchy
and caught on hair that is too coarse, too
bushy, too flat and uneven, the wave
too wide, the sides too slow, my nostrils
too dry. what I wouldn't give for a mirror
to freshen my face, run fingers through
my hair, straighten my part, pat the
curls, bluff the fluff, line my eyes, wine
my cheeks, wine your last look at me.

make no mistake

When she came for her money,
I said, I kept the 10 spot because
I cleaned the closet you didn't.
I washed the floor you didn't.
I scraped the pots, changed
the sheets, polishing, polishing.

The sills are deep with
the dust you'll swipe next time,
the winter of mud I saw only after
you had gone. I stared at it for a while
because I wanted to believe you had not
stolen from me with next times,
strutting past the oven still warm with lies.

65

Terminal Moraine

When my daughter asks about my childhood,
I say it is a threshold she cannot cross.
But it is no more mysterious than my yard
where pebbles are tossed toward despair like the poor.

I remember being driven
through a thick wood.
Maybe it was not yet dawn.
Maybe it was wartime.
Maybe I was taken to strangers.
It felt as if the road was lined with tigers.
I got sick and an uncle came for me,
driving the only car in the family.
Every year I was sent away. Every year I got sick.
Every year that distant wood closed over me.
But not every year did my uncle come for me.

The thought of this returns the way the ocean
splashed on her, cold at the knees.
It is Rockaway Beach.
She is pregnant with me,
beautiful but ungainly in the picture,
circumscribed by a tarnished metal frame.
She said she loved home life,
but she never owned maternity clothes.
She was always somewhere else
Or painting in her attic room.
She did what he'd let her in those days.

He never called her by her first name
or wore the wedding band that
joined her to whatever canvas
she sketched alone late at night.
Some of this I have already forgotten.

Somewhere in my story my daughter
accepts the benign stretch marks of that time
that still leaves me somewhere soft.

my version

for Howard Nemerov

To be the wife of the artist
I must be curtain and backdrop
but most of all, scrim.
I must withstand long stories
about Red Smith and wartime London,
ramblings about Danté and Don Giovanni.

I use his last name, plain enough,
but it doesn't get me far.
At parties I glance around to see
what he's doing, not to see
if he's all right. He is always all right.
Somebody is always taking care of him.

Every day I wrap two pale cookies,
an apple, cored, precut, and brought back
together with clear plastic as on lunch lines,
a sandwich with one slice of yellow
cheese in a square plastic container,
and a bag of chips. Every day.

And I am grateful that
there aren't two like him in the house.
What would get done?
Who would dish out lunch?
Still the dogs?
Unpeople the place?

I talk about bread. Will it be potatoes or rice?
Who will have tea?

I wake up and doze again. One eyelid droops.
My pupils are uneven.
My vision sometimes clouds.
The doctor says calcium is deposited
on my retinas. I don't know why.

reading the dipstick

Did I make myself worse the pain that knots up in the fever you removed
has grown back and hardened when you told me it wouldn't you lied
there is nothing beautiful here my legs are crooked and sizzling out of
control I take chalky pills to tide me over when the medicine wears off
and the pain shudders through my hips like an electric charge until I
realize that my body cannot return I am stuck with it for all the dread and
mistakes it lodges the sale is over and all were final I have given up
caring whether I am the source
or the delta
or how much
of me lies
above the
Arctic Circle
I am only
good for
standing
in the corner
of the down-
stairs hall
made for
wet umbrellas
or a bucket
of sand
on an
icy day
that is
thrown
into orbit
to protest
everyone
from
falling
but
me

Matters of Course

It could have been me recuperating,
receiving flowers and phone calls.
We both had stained for months,
unmistakable but not menopausal.
We both went in at the same time,
I to Luke, she to Lutheran.

Mine was not a mere cyst that a d&c
would have taken care of,
but a tumor that grows on the uterine wall.
It called for surgery as dark as birth itself,
serious, but not serious enough to enjoy

whole memos written about bringing her mail.
The privilege of the sick,
to come downstairs once a day,
to be driven around, especially once she
started treatments. Implants, she said.
By the time they did the first, she didn't
need the second. But they performed
the hysterectomy anyway,
as a matter of course.

Never mind the vacancy,
the threads of hair that grow at her lip,
the skin tabs that spread like tubers.
She was proud of the incision
she mapped on her robe.

the tissue I thought was sucked out
like unwanted dust. No, she said.
Muscle and membrane are too big to pass
naturally, as an infant.
How such bankruptcy can be
larger than the largest newborn,
its breadth and spine.
But you can't tell under her house coat,
good for housework and changes like this one.

When it rains violently red, I make a slip of the tongue but not enough to jail me

So you went out without me,
and you tell me you're lonely.
You wipe your nose along the sleeve
of a story no one believes.

I'm going to drive the shit 20 hours
and who cares: my setting at a truck stop,
full serve, take a shower,
sleep at the wheel,
cross myself crossing the Susquehanna,
squeeze left
at Wheeling, West Virginia

Where I'll keep my nose forward,
my neck stretched up,
and my eyes on freedom.

Where I'll walk into Calamity Café
at the heat of the day,
wearing sandals, a shrunken
tee shirt, and short shorts,
with my hips swinging available.

Where I'll stroll by the Y M C A,
people coming out with gym bags
and towels slung around
their lives, brown and muscular.
I'll just walk past the hard-hats,
gawking from their latest bricks
and following me with their hands
'cause here it's anybody's ball game.

Where I won't worry about
leaving tracks on the cement.
I'll forget my watch and walk
just headlong out. My own single self,
like any other person without the clutter
of babies, without a man with
warts on his legs.
I'll overdress and pretend
I'm going somewhere,
maybe lunch, an appointment
somewhere special.

To remember:

if I have removed my freckles
taken my calcium
if my teeth feel rounded and safe
if no pimples grow under my arm
no curious itch assaults me
if I have broken no fingernail
hidden in the cave of my groin
if I have unfrozen dinner
scratched my scab
if I have celebrated, consecrated
if I have buried my enemies
flossed my teeth and rinsed.

something tugs at me

I don't remember what it was,
just that it was about having children,
because I wanted to be a woman.
I pick them up and warm them
with the insides of my arms.
So long as they are with me,
there can be no harm.

What would make me throw
my body over them,
cradle them in blankets,
spread my nerve roots,
wrap them in muscle,
pass them to you?
What would make me steal, kill,
climb an electrified fence?

I will die with my eyes open.
I will pack my things in bundles
like paragraphs that
last only one generation
and belong to my children.
I marveled at the way
they marveled at mountains,
the glacial streets and parks.
Now it's their turn to watch
their children and clap and sing.

Amusements

40 Fascinations at Yaddo

For a moment I think the idea
is to disappear.
The East House is west.
The director's house turns out to be
cords of wood stacked behind a racetrack.
The secondary road becomes
an overgrown, impassable trail that
narrows to a path and ends abruptly at a fence.
The wrought iron gates have no fence.
The wire fence has no gate.
The wooden gates have no woods.

I find the bike keys but not
the bikes. Or the pool. The keys
to the towels intended to dangle
above the pool door now poke out from
the side of a shed to the left of
a door that can't be locked anyway.
I never find the tennis court
but hear the wap of the ball.

The fountains come on when they
are in the mood,
usually in the rain, usually at night,
rarely on weekdays, never on weekends.
The goldfish are direct descendants of
those starting up the bowl in '34.

Through a shrub at stage right,
the rose garden moves
ever so slightly every day.

The public lawn is marked
Private Area Beyond Here.
Should someone ask, I can say
I belong, like the bugle calls
made of bells.

Pollen from the fir trees
sprinkles saffron on the salad
and makes imperative
mowing the lawn before meals.

A school bus delivers the mail.
The Yaddo shadow hammers
copper on the roof,
heavy foots it on the stairs.
Sleds whip down the bannister.
The housekeeper shortsheets my bed.

I have lost my sense of direction
but remember my sky. I pull it down
at night for privacy when I'm as tired
as the John Deere dreaming in the shed
where the bikes should be but aren't.

Walks tend not to be,
along with the Tiffany sconces
and Paranisi prints.

The social director plans
a no-pressure Talent Night.
Nonparticipation is voluntary
with an explanation.

In my lunch pail is a note
stating that it is respectable to
wear New York and know people.
The flying ants and I have come to terms.

Coupons

Seeking 25 words or less,
must be serious,
spontaneous and successful,
peach protected but would be willing
to consider unscented, thin scented, thick,
think Light Days, Long Sures and Natural
with generous, old-fashioned security,
tabbed or winged, poised or pursed,
interested in meeting The Freez Family:
the Carefrees, StayFrees, New Freedoms,

Or the any-member-once-removed Freez Sisters,
looking for honest and sincere Anydays,
sheer with soft sorb and
a sense of humor. Should be unattached,
attractive, and financially deodorized.

Moisture strip and lock trying to find
Shift B relationship before autumn, enjoys
Playtexes plays saxes to pay taxes from Tampaxes
Texas or sexes, the original
patented round tip with flexible,
gentle slide and baking soda freshness
for dependable leak-proof companion.

Friend in a tall slim fit searches
for someone with similar
Ultimates, fun loving and forever wild,
the super-for-supper maxi with or
without wings, thighs, breasts, cajun or plain,
Ultra Longs plus new night napkins
with dining, dancing, movies for lasting,
confidential comfort with a Dri-Weave
through Central Park.

You're always ready for
wrap around overnights for which
you are Carefree and curved,
Superplus Supertabbed taxi or maxi.
The Stay-Dri system between home and work,
your place or mine.
As Always, will consider a swap.

Ipecac for Teaching

You keep me waiting.
You put me off.
Have a little respect.
Phone me when you're supposed to.
Order my parking sticker
and deliver my grade book.
Knock on my door and
work around *my* schedule.
I want an office not a closet
and a nod of appreciation.
Can't you recognize quality
when you see it?

I know all about department chairs,
with their Norton Reader rising
on the shelf like a cathedral.
They swivel around with their
Neiman Marcus ennui
and talk columns and arches
and the drama of course objectives.
Don't put on airs when I have
the degree and you are a quonset hut
just because you got there first.
Book me early and give me prime time.
And don't read your rules to me,
because I don't take orders from turkey
and mashed potatoes in a tin cup.

What Would Jackie Take?

Would Jackie take Wisk for washing bras?
Would she pack dental floss or Stimudents?
A sewing kit courtesy of Days Inn?
Would she take Wash 'n Dries? A fanny pack
So she can enter museums and
keep her passport and small change?

Would Jackie pack nail glue for patching split ends?
Would she get a haircut a week before
and a touch up at her widow's peak?

Would Jackie need Sucrets, Pepto, Gelusil?
Ear plugs to mute the babies crying
all night in economy class?
And twistems and plastic bags? Packs of tissues
she saved from the Red Roof Inn?
And how many Long Days, Maxi Thins, and OBs?

Would Jackie take mousse, hair spray, the free shampoos
from the Hyatt that she can discard as she uses?
Should she take 3-minute conditioner,
so while it's working she can wash between her toes?
Should she bother with a shower cap,
blue daisies on mermaid plastic?

Would she cut her toe nails and bleach
the hair above her mouth two nights
before she leaves, so that one night before
she can shave under her arms? Razor or electric?
And how high on her legs should she go?
How much of them would show on the beach at Kamakura?

Should she take photos or buy postcards?
Should she take movies or slides? And how many rolls?
And who would carry the zoom and change the film?
A bird book? Binoculars? Fodor's or Frommer's?
Would she carry Lipton's and a coil heater
in case the tea is green?

Would Jackie wait in line for traveler's checks
while her credit is verified?
And how much money should she buy?
And how many singles would she need for tips?

What about sensible walking shoes,
thongs, and dress sneakers?
Should Jackie wear a Greek scarf in Osaka?
Take Tang to disguise the foreign water and
sunglasses big as bulbs to disguise herself?
Should she wave to her children from the runway?

The Hubbard in Modern Poetry

Here at hermitage hollow the
wholesome history of homemade bread and
old cupboard mother's cherry jelly hikes
to grandmother's hallowed house
where no consonants scrape our throat
on the hickoried hearth.
Warm bread wafts on wings.
Hollies hock, hams hang,
holidays sing honey butter,
help gingham onto sugar mapled
mason jars, ball jars, bell jars.
Bell choirs glisten at the church.
The snow is hoed by humptied hands while
her heritage quilts our humble hostess
sprinkling, trinkling, trickling,
tickling a heaven of tollhouse.
In the heathered rocking chair
next to its heaving hassock,
our Laura Ashley life hums.
We heart health and happiness. Hymns
herbal our hair, far from harm and hazard.
Oh, hear the Hansel time-honored.

Junk Mail

Later that day she picked up the mail and found a strange box addressed to her/ nothing she had ordered/ no return address/no identifying marks/why do record clubs, book clubs, cheese and chocolate clubs insist on sending freebies/ Or did she accidentally throw something away that said: If you fail to send back this form, you will receive the first of 86 volumes of the rise and fall of the phonetic system of Old English/And you won't be billed until after Christmas/ Then, if she opens it, she is instantly responsible for resealing it/ taking it to the post office/ and what's worse/ paying for the privilege of returning it to a place from which it never should have come.

She reached for a pair of scissors/she hesitated/ she took out a steak knife/ she put it down/all she'd have to do is keep the package intact/ write on it: Refused, in bold black letters, and slip it into the mail box/ that's what Elaine's in-laws did when they received a New Year's card from her after a quarrel/ didn't she remember a parcel post box just around the corner/but this is a Cinderella story/ what the hell, she said/ she'd take a chance/she ran one blade of the scissors squarely down the center of the wide brown tape/ she opened the box/lo and behold/ beneath some paper, a book, and a gift besides, she exclaimed/from one daughter/ for hospitality, bed, crowded quarters, hot and warm running conversation/ now to the good fortune/now to the thank you/ now to the read.

chance music

Thank you for coming
I am pleased you are
Pleased
To know
I don't think we've met
I'm glad we
Thank you for listening
For seeking me out
For knowing
It feels like
I just do what I do
Does that make sense?
Your face is familiar
Your name is
I didn't put the two
There are lots of
Good
Meeting you
I say that because
Yes, you can get it here
Or there
It's hard to say
I appreciate
I'm flattered that
You chose to be
Nice
To see so many
It's good to be
Old fashioned
It's kind of you
To stay and listen
To take the wonderful
Time to
Thank you for enjoying
Is that the right word?
For understanding
The ordinary

I even appreciate
Your going
Out of your way
To be here
To hear me
I don't know
Quite what
I am
A little
Do come again
I am honored that
It is delightful

URGENT

Directors, Heads, Managers, Leaders

Stop Her
Sign Nothing
Give Her No Time Or Inclination
Authorize No Budget, Supplies, Keys To The Lockers,
No Access To Fact Or Fancy

When She Knocks, Close Your Door
Don't Answer Your Phone Evenings Or Weekends
She Will Take Your Money, Your Job
She's Hot, A Twister
Contain The Fire. Get The Hoses
Ladders, Rope, Masks, Germ Warfare

Air. Give Us Air.

Vital Statistics

The personnel director said:
No woman in this company
is promoted with a swagger
in her mouth, rings in the side
of her nose. We reward the little lady
with the blazer and the string tie.
Now that's a woman for you,
feminine but not quite,
Jewish but not Joan Rivers,
black but not Shange,
who does not ask for raises,
who minds her own business
because she's here
to work for the rest of us,
the best of us.

So I wrote
Dear Father Superior:
I would like returned to my office
the phone that was removed without
warning the day I was sick.
I'll have back my bulletin board
that was confiscated when you moved my office
to the back and scribbled all over my pride,
and we ran out of good feelings.
And it disappeared along with my stamp pad
and my self-respect.
I want back my typewriter that you so cannily
borrow every few days to remind me that
I still work for you and everything here is yours.
And the civil rights purchased
for me when you liked me better
because I was tentative and nondescript.
And while I'm thinking of it,
I'll take back the bonus you swiped
when you prayed I wouldn't last, and

my desk that you rifled through to see
if I'd left any accomplishments lying around.
I'll keep my own achievements, thank you.

And you ain't heard nothing yet.
I'm going to march you into the vps and report
that you lie, you thieve.
Not only have you repossessed my title
and shanghaied my space,
you have picked my pockets, rigged the deck,
and walked off with my words.

When I'm through with you,
we're going to trade places. And
I'll have 4 phones, 3 secretaries,
2 office boys, kitchen privileges,
conference calling, windows, drapes,
and your more bang-for-the-buck.
And don't make fists at me in your pockets,
'cause if you keep messing with me,
you're gonna find yourself in a poem.

Photo by Jill Gussow

Alice G. Brand is Professor of English at SUNY Brockport where she teaches courses in creative writing and composition studies. Her poetry has been published in *New Letters, 13th Moon, Phoebe, The Cape Rock, Nimrod, Minnesota Review, Kalliope, Literary Review, River Styx, Confrontation, Paintbrush, americas review, South Florida Poetry Review, Bellingham Review*, and *Kansas Quarterly;* and essays and fiction published in the *New England Quarterly, Kalliope*, and *The New York Times.*

Brand's poetry has been awarded first prize in competitions sponsored by the Midwest Region Poetry Society of America, the *Sing Heavenly Muse!* collective, and the *Wildwood Journal* for the title poem of her second collection, *Studies on Zone* (University of Missouri, BkMk Press). Her first collection, *As It Happens,* was published by Wampeter Press. She is a three-time Yaddo fellow.